SMOOTH SELLING FOREVER

Charting Your Company's Course for Predictable and Sustainable Sales Growth

CRAIG LOWDER

ISBN-10: 1-941870-54-6
ISBN-13: 978-1-941870-54-9
Library of Congress Control Number: 2016934260

Designed by Joni McPherson, www.mcphersongraphics.com

INDIE BOOKS INTERNATIONAL, LLC
2424 VISTA WAY, SUITE 316
OCEANSIDE, CA 92054
www.indiebooksintl.com

Contents

Section I

Pick a Problem: Wasted Opportunities or Stalled Growth?

"It is not the ship so much as the skillful sailing that assures the prosperous voyage."

– George William Curtis, American author and civil service reformer, 1824-1892

Typically a company's sales challenges can be reduced to one of two problems. The first is the ineffective handling of prospective deals resulting in squandered sales opportunities. The second challenge is a scarcity of qualified prospective deals that results in a disappointing lack of anticipated growth.

Chapter One

The Call to Have Predictable and Sustainable Sales Growth

Ed McConaghay, the CEO of Telident, had a problem they did not prepare him for at West Point or the Harvard Business School. He knew about battle plans and business plans, but what he really needed was a strategic sales plan.

Before being acquired by Teltronics Inc. in May of 2000, Telident, Inc. was a privately held company engaged in the design, manufacture, and marketing of proprietary hardware and software systems, which provide the exact location of a 911 telephone call to the emergency dispatcher at the public safety answering point who receives the call.

When I joined the organization as the vice president of sales, the cost of sales was out of control. The first challenge was the company only had a small sales team with limited bandwidth responsible for generating their own leads. The second challenge was once a lead was generated, the sales reps were flying all over the country to sell a product that took a minimum of three face-to-face sales calls to close. The third challenge was a low lead-to-sale conversion rate, due to the fact the company was not leveraging its technology channel partners to open doors and assist with the sale.

It did not take a West Point graduate to determine this was no way to win the war. A different approach was in order.

A smooth selling approach was needed and fast. The strategic sales plan we put in place emphasized selling through channel partners rather than trying to sell directly to the clients of these channel partners. Our solution was to make our 911 product an add-on module that the channel partners could sell when they sold an on-premise telephone system/PBX.

The sales team was comprised of good people, but the wrong kind of people. Since we did not have the right people to support the sales strategy, we hired people who did. The sales team was made up of hunters, but what we needed was farmers. Hunters are good at selling direct, but are not good at working with channel partners. The hunters' egos and need to control the sale get in the way.

Next we put a sales process, activity- and results-based performance metrics, and a sales training program in place. The theme was to create a culture of sales enablement.

In the first year, we added four strategic channel relationships that generated $1.8 million in new revenue, total sales increased by 78 percent, and productivity per sales rep increased by 65 percent.

Top Twelve Reasons Why Sales are not Growing as Expected

The challenges at Telident were not unusual. Over the past three decades I have studied dozens and dozens of small to mid-size companies where the selling was not smooth. Patterns began to emerge as to why sales were not growing as expected.

Based on my research, the following list of reasons is provided in reverse rank order, from number twelve to number one.

12. No annual performance reviews.

An annual performance review forces a manager to sit down and evaluate performance. This is the time to set goals for the following year. Then progress should be tracked and discussed minimally on a quarterly basis if not monthly. This also lays the foundation for performance improvement and, if necessary, termination.

11. **Over reliance on sales team to generate leads.**
    Having sales reps fend for themselves when it comes to finding leads is an ineffective approach. While sales reps should always be on the lookout for good prospects, there should be an automated, digital lead-generation and lead-nurturing program in place to feed them qualified leads.

10. **Limited, ineffective sales skills training; sales mentoring is non-existent.**
    A sales leader should travel with each sales rep regularly–at least monthly–to determine their competency. With that, knowledge and skills training can be customized to fit each rep's needs. The best training involves ongoing coaching and mentoring in addition to formal training sessions. Role-playing is an

excellent way to test a sales rep's ability to apply what he or she has been taught. Practice improves performance.

9. **Compensation plan doesn't incent desired behavior.**
   What gets rewarded gets done. The comp plan should provide the right activity- and results-based incentives. An effective comp plan is a win-win for the sales rep and the company. Another question to consider: will it help attract the right salespeople?

8. **No customer relationship management (CRM) system.**
   A first step is to determine the proper application of CRM for the team. CRM is not one size fits all, and should be customized to match the company's sales processes, sales support structure, and sales reporting requirements. This is the single repository for all sales activity and results reporting. The proper implementation of a CRM system enables multiple departments to see the status of sales activities and deal progression.

7. **Sales message doesn't differentiate from the competition.**
   The company's sales message must distinguish the company from the competition by communicating unique value. To accomplish this, the message must be: (1) important to the prospect, (2) unique to your company, and (3) easy to defend against competitive attack. There are three messaging musts: it must be *simple,* it must be presented from the *customer's point-of-view,* and it must be *memorable.*

6. **Sales team is not staffed properly.**
   The sales team must be led by a sales manager who is focused on building highly effective sales reps versus securing individual sales to achieve significant and sustainable results. There needs to be a proper structure to maximize sales, such as outside versus inside reps, reps that are hunters versus reps that are farmers, and direct sales versus indirect sales channel support reps.

5. **No short-term and/or long-term sales pipeline and forecasting tool.**

A sales pipeline and forecasting tool provides a bottom-up view for use by the company to forecast future sales, align costs with expected revenues, and accurately predict cash flow. Monitoring the sales pipeline is one of the most important duties of a sales manager.

4. **No weekly scheduled sales meetings for the group and one-to-one.**
   These meetings should be a learning experience designed to share success stories, what's working and what's not working, as well as to identify and resolve issues that are getting in the way of making sales. These meetings are the foundation of effective coaching and mentoring. Each member of the sales team should know what is expected of them each week. The sales leader should make sure everyone comes prepared to report on their expected deliverables.

3. **Sales metrics are not clearly defined.**
   Attention must be paid to how a company is keeping score of sales *activities* and *results*. This is how a company sets the proper performance levels it desires and provides a common scorekeeping system for what is

defined as good and bad. Furthermore, this is how to determine future success before it is too late.

2. **No defined sales processes.**
   Each step of a company's sales processes must be clearly stated and documented. This creates a common language and understanding of sales success. It is vitally important to define checkpoints for each step in the sales process.

1. **No detailed sales plan that is understood by the entire sales team.**
   The number one reason holding companies back from smooth selling is the lack of a sales plan understood by all. Remember this business adage? "The probability of hitting your goal is much greater if you have one." A business must know where it wants to go and when and how it wants to get there. A written plan must be created that includes three critical elements: (1) sales strategy, (2) sales support/enablement systems, and (3) sales organization structure and people (all of which will be discussed later in this book in chapters four, five, and six). The plan must

include clear deadlines and accountability for executing each and every plan component. This must be clearly stated in writing. No fuzzy thinking allowed.

Smooth Selling from the Beginning

Most of the stories in this book are wasted opportunity or stalled growth stories. But this also works from the get-go. When a company is in startup mode, then there is the opportunity to start smooth selling from the beginning. That was the case in 2002 for Gary Schafer, a serial entrepreneur with an MBA from Northwestern and a pedigree from McKinsey Consulting. In 2002 he co-founded and became the CEO of SIVOX Technologies, a Chicago area developer of simulation-based eLearning software solutions targeting Fortune 500 companies with inbound and outbound customer call centers.

When there is no market, a company needs to create one. SIVOX provided software and support services designed to help companies better recruit and train their call-center agents. The company's system, used in about eighty call centers nationwide, enabled call-center agents to practice their call-handling skills through interactive simulations.

As the vice president of sales and marketing, I participated in the launch of this new company. We designed and branded the product as a prepackaged software solution. With the strategy in place, the next task was to hire and train a sales force that could fill the pipeline.

The results were sales of $1.9 million with two Fortune 100 companies (MCI and Sprint) and a $20 million-plus sales pipeline within nine months of launch. We also won the Chicago Software Association's 2003 Early Stage Investment Conference Business Plan Award.

Smooth Selling Ahead

What is smooth selling? Think of the successful America's Cup yachting teams as the metaphor.

The America's Cup is the oldest international sporting trophy, an ornate sterling-silver pitcher awarded to the winner of the America's Cup match races. The trophy was originally awarded in 1851 for a race around the Isle of Wight in England, which was won by the schooner America. The trophy was renamed the America's Cup after the yacht and was donated to the New York Yacht Club with terms that made it available for perpetual international competition.

The history and prestige associated with the America's Cup attracts the world's top yacht designers, sailors, and crews. In addition, the race could not happen without the involvement of wealthy sponsors and partners. It is a test not only of sailing skill and boat design, but also of fund-raising and management skills.

What it takes to win the America's Cup yacht race can readily be likened to winning in sales.

Assess. The first step is to assess. In sailing you have to assess if you have the right technology and people. Yacht design and finding the right sailors is a constantly evolving science. In business you have to assess the four critical areas of sales operations: strategy, methodology, performance metrics, and people.

Design. In yachting next comes boat and sail design. That might mean a twelve-meter yacht, a ninety-foot multihull yacht, or a wing-sail catamaran. In business the second step is to design the right sales plan: sales strategy, sales enablement/support systems, and people. Different challenges call for different sales approaches. For instance, do you need a sales team of hunters or farmers or both?

Deploy. A third step is to deploy. The America's Cup sailors are some of the best trained athletes in the world. Before the sailing races begin there has been rigorous training and preparation. In business the third step is to deploy the sales team and support systems. They need to know what the strategy is and what is expected of them to win.

Execute. Finally comes the execution. Yacht races are not won on paper, they are won in the water. While technology and strategy are important, the yacht captain must get the most from the crew in order to win. To succeed in business, the execution of the sales plan must be properly managed. The goal is to ensure the sales plan is executed as effectively as possible and that the sales team adopts the necessary sales processes and reporting systems. Like in sailing, this calls for leadership.

When it all comes together, that is smooth selling. I know because I have seen it happen time and time again. While the America's Cup metaphor helps explain the concept, rest assured this is not an all theory and no real-world application book. A pragmatic look at smooth selling is the focus of the next chapter.

Chapter Two

The Quest for Smooth Selling

Smooth selling is what enables small and mid-size business leaders to generate significant, predictable, and sustainable sales growth. Based in the science of selling, when applied correctly and managed vigilantly smooth selling produces revenue results in a systematic fashion.

The main message of this book is this: Selling is a science that must be artfully executed. Like any other science, there are scientific sales principles to follow. Much like the field of medicine, there needs to be diagnosis before prescription. The diagnosis, while artfully detected, is based on a body of knowledge. After a prescription there needs to be intense monitoring of the patient. In medicine they call it the vital signs. In sales we call it the sales metrics.

Here is the good news. The dream of creating a smooth-selling system that will generate significant, predictable, and sustainable sales growth is obtainable; however, you must make the effort to get the knowledge of how others have done it and then apply that knowledge.

The Added Benefits of Smooth Selling

The primary benefit of adopting a smooth selling approach is to generate significant, predictable, and sustainable sales growth. Here is a rundown of the key other benefits:

Shorter Sales Cycle. There is an adage in sales that time kills deals. The longer it takes a deal to close, the less likely it will actually close. Smooth selling seeks to close more deals by shortening the buying process.

Higher Lead-to-Sales Conversion Rates. Leads are like at-bats in baseball. Increasing your batting average means converting more of the leads into sales. Small increases in conversion rates can have a huge impact on gross revenue.

Larger Transaction Sizes. A smooth selling approach helps the sales team focus not just on the number of deals, but also the size of the deal. Increasing transaction size can greatly increase revenue growth.

Higher Gross Profit Margins. A culprit for lower gross profit margins is discounting. Many company leaders have bought into the belief that discounting is the only way to get the business. Smooth selling seeks to minimize discounting and raise gross profit margins.

Longer Sales Employee Retention and Less Turnover. Most companies report they have difficulties attracting and retaining quality sales professionals and sales managers. Sales employees like to play on a team that is a winner and has its act together. The relationship between sales professional and manager cannot be overstated.

More Cost-Effective Lead Generation. One of the tragedies in business is the amount of sales leads that are wasted. Another tragedy is when leads are gathered in an inefficient manner.

Better ROI on Marketing. By eliminating sales lead waste, the natural result is an increased return on investment from marketing.

Less Business Owner and Sales Leader Stress. Overall, smooth selling reduces stress on the business leaders. When owners have a sales team they can count on, they can focus their attention on other areas of the business. When sales leaders have a sales team they can count on, they can produce more predictable and sustainable sales results.

The Winthrop Resources Story

John Morgan, CEO of Winthrop Resources Corporation of Minnesota, is a big Warren Buffett fan.

How big? In 1999 the Berkshire Hathaway Inc. billionaire investor auctioned off his twenty-year-old wallet for $210,000 as part of an effort to raise funds for an Omaha, Nebraska, charity. In the wallet: a stock tip. The winning bidder, Morgan, said he would reveal the stock's name to individuals who gave $1,000 or more to the charity. *The Wall Street Journal* reported that about 30 people forked over the money.

This is the same Morgan who once bought a portrait of Warren Buffett for $100,000, also for charity. Then in 2011 Morgan bought Buffett's childhood home – where the future Oracle of Omaha lived until age six – and plans to sell it on eBay for $150,100, the *Omaha World-Herald* reported. There were thirteen bids for the house, which was built in 1923 from a Sears Roebuck kit, and Morgan said he was prepared to pay more if necessary.

I had the pleasure to work with Morgan and bring the smooth selling concepts to Winthrop Resources as enterprise national sales manager. Over a ten-month period we developed and launched a strategic alliance program that generated $12 million in new sales, along with seventeen new accounts. We also launched a financial marketing program that generated $4.2 million in new sales, along with twelve new business partnerships.

Here's how we did it. Founded in 1982, Winthrop Resources had a singular focus: leasing information technology and capital equipment from all manufacturers, vendors, and value added resellers to businesses across a range of industries. When a company buys information technology and capital equipment in the $250,000 to $20 million range there are two big decisions: what product do we buy and how do we pay for it. We provided several lease financing options that allowed the companies to buy more and leverage the cash-flow advantages of leasing.

When I arrived and assessed the situation it was clear that lease financing was viewed as a highly transactional business, and the focus was on finding technology and capital-equipment buyers that would consider lease financing. Obtaining informal leads from companies like Oracle was not handled in a strategic fashion.

Morgan supported my big idea to develop a formal strategic alliance program with technology and capital equipment sellers like Oracle, SAP, and IBM to help their sales reps close the sale by providing a host of lease financing options. This took a formalized sales approach to train the reps of the technology companies to close more sales and bigger sales using lease financing as a sales tool. While companies were familiar with the concept of lease financing the hardware, we showed them how software and professional services could be bundled together with the hardware in the lease.

For purchases under $250,000, such as new point-of-sales systems (the modern electronic descendent of the old cash register) for McDonalds, we showed them how they could give franchisees more lease options. Partnerships require problem solving. For instance, we agreed to hold on to the leases, not bundle and sell them to a third party, so if there was a problem they would deal with us.

Smooth Selling's Thirty-Year Successful Track Record

If we are about to embark on a smooth selling voyage, you need to know who the skipper is. Okay, so here is the truth about me, straight up.

I didn't go to Harvard, I didn't go to Stanford, and you won't find a bunch of letters after my name. I once went as far as having MBA on my business card, but you won't find it there anymore.

Mine was a blue-collar family just outside the rust belt, where I learned that it's not only what you know, but how you apply it. I learned a couple of other important lessons back then that still serve me today.

One is that teamwork is a critical component of success anywhere–whether you are playing shortstop on a baseball field, crewing a yacht in the America's Cup, or navigating the challenges of the global economy. That's why as president of my own sales consulting firm, I only work with clients who are willing to listen, think, and contribute to their own development and their company's success. Success comes to a team, not individuals.

The second is nothing beats experience. I've been mentored by some of the best in the business – people like Brad Sugars, Verne Harnish, Larry Wilson, Jeffrey Gitomer, and Keith Cunningham – but I've really learned the best teacher is experience.

And I've had my share. During my thirty-plus year career as a sales manager and consultant, I have worked with over fifty B2B and B2C companies, increasing their following year sales by 22 to 142 percent. Some of my most memorable experiences include:

- leading the turnaround of a failing communications technology reseller, turning a $156,000 loss in year one to a profit of $453,000 in year three;
- developing and launching two marketing programs that generated $16.2 million in new business in one year for a financial services company;
- increasing a software company's sales from $9.1 million to $24.1 million in two years; and,
- launching and growing a business unit to $16 million in revenue over eight years, and

positioning it for a sale, along with its parent company, to a Fortune 100 company.

But it has not all been smooth selling. Through it all I've seen the good and the bad, and, frankly, learned more from the bad than the good. There have been storms that tested me. It is a real-world perspective that guides my work with growing companies today.

That is the same perspective that guides this book: the secret of smooth selling is to develop and execute a comprehensive strategic sales plan. Nothing else will do. Most companies only strike at this goal with half measures. To strike with full force, a company must chart the following course:

- Develop a sales strategy, from market segments to buying processes
- Determine the right sales channels for a go-to-market plan
- Design an optimum sales and sales support organization
- Create the systems and tools of a solid sales infrastructure

A Sample E-Mail

The following is an actual testimonial used with the CEO's permission (but not his name). The numbers tell the story as to what can happen with a smooth selling approach.

Good morning Craig,

Here is a review for Jan-June 2015 and July-Dec 2015 for new business since we implemented the sales process in July 2015. See attached spreadsheet for year-to-date info. Highlights are huge! This is for new business.

Period	Average new face-to-face calls	Average # of quotes	Average quoted $	Average # of orders	Average $ order won	Average success ratio
1st six months	11	15	$184,680	1	$9,138	7%
2nd six months	23	31	$290,115	7	$42,413	20%
Percentage delta	+200%	+200%	+157%	+656%	+464%	+285%

It demonstrates the need to keep sales people out of office pursuing new accounts. The numbers tell the story.

Sincerely,

Where We Are Sailing To

For businesses that are struggling with the rough waters of too many opportunities or stalled growth, there is a way out to the calm seas of smooth selling forever. The secret is gaining the knowledge of how other small and mid-size companies have done it and then executing. The following section details exactly how to do it.

SECTION II

The Smooth Selling System

"If one does not know to which port one is sailing, no wind is favorable"

–LUCIUS ANNAEUS SENECA, ROMAN STATESMAN (4 BC- 65 AD)

Actions must be taken to create the foundation for significant, predictable, and sustainable sales growth. The key to smooth selling is strategy, systems, and people.

Chapter 3

The Smooth Selling System

Call it the XYZ Technology Corporation. As the old *Dragnet* police show would say: "The story is true, but the names have been changed to protect the innocent."

Once upon a time I was recruited by private equity firm to help turnaround a company's failing sales, marketing, and customer service operations. The objective was to reposition the company for acquisition.

XYZ Tech Corp. was a $175 million reseller of network communications hardware, professional design consulting, and technical support services. Profitability had gone in the tank so the investors brought in a new CEO and me to stop the bleeding of red ink and get the company back in the black.

In its most advanced form, selling should be a scientifically managed process. There is no room for guesswork and hunches. Careful thought needs to go into planning, implementation, and evaluation. Smooth selling is always broken down into the four-step process introduced in chapter one.

Assess. The first step in sales planning is to assess. This entails a detailed assessment of the four critical areas of sales operations: strategy, methodology, performance metrics, and organization. At XYZ Tech Corp. this included sales operation audits that looked at sales processes, sales forecasting, sales quotas, sales performance metrics, sales organization structure, and people assessment, and then a gap analysis of where the company needed to be.

Design. The second step in sales planning is to design. At XYZ Tech Corp. we designed a new sales engagement model, reengineered sales processes, and established a value proposition for each of the company's six professional service offerings.

Deploy. The third step in sales planning is to deploy. At XYZ Corp. that included a sales team reorganization and the introduction of a new customer relationship management (CRM) system to track sales activity, as well as results. At this stage the focus is on talent assessment, recruiting, hiring and training systems, sales processes, sales support systems, and performance metrics.

Execute. And finally, to succeed, the execution of the sales plan must be properly managed. The goal is to ensure the sales plan is executed as effectively as possible and that the sales team adopts the necessary sales processes, performance metrics, and reporting requirements. At XYZ Tech Corp. I personally led the efforts to rollout and monitor the new strategy, systems, and people.

Here were the results at XYZ Tech Corp. We completely turned the ship around. Over a four-month period we achieved 122 percent of sales plan, increased gross profit margins by 12 percent, and reduced sales expenses by 16 percent. Additionally, as a member of the due-diligence team I was intimately involved with the successful sale of the company.

Pop Quiz: Test Your Smooth Selling Seaworthiness

The time has come to assess your organization and your role as a business leader. Answer the following dozen questions to the best of your ability.

Question	**Yes**	**No**	**I don't know**
Have you traveled with each of your sales reps in the past year to see what they are doing, how they are doing it, and if they are performing as expected?			
Does your company hold weekly scheduled team sales meetings and one-to-ones with each member of the sales team?			
Does your company have an annual budget for sales skills training?			
Does every member of your sales team have an assigned annual sales quota?			
Does your company have a documented sales process and use an automated sales forecasting tool?			
Does your company have documented results-based and activity-based sales performance metrics?			
Does your company conduct annual sales performance reviews?			
Does your company use a CRM system that has been customized to support your sales processes and reporting needs?			
Does your sales incentive compensation plan drive the desired sales behavior?			
Is your sales organization staffed properly?			

Question	Yes	No	I don't know
Does your company have a sales message that differentiates your company from the competition and minimizes price competition?			
Does your company have a detailed sales plan that is understood and is being followed by everyone on the sales team?			

Your Selling Seaworthiness Score _____# of Yes Answers

Assessing Your Score

10-12 Yes. Bravo. Well done, skipper. You and your crew are doing a great deal correct. This puts you in the top 10 percent of all companies.

7-9 Yes. Congratulations, but mind the helm. While not smooth selling yet, you are making solid progress. But what are the gaps? This puts you in the better than average group.

4-6 Yes. All hands on deck. Your score is not good, but not unusual. Typically this means you have great opportunities for improvement. Start by plugging the biggest leaks.

1-3 Yes. Ahoy, your boat may be sinking. I wish I could say the only place to go is up. But in truth you could be sinking to the bottom. Take some comfort that about 30 percent of companies are there with you, and this book can help you make things shipshape.

The Fujitsu Business Communication Systems Story

What I liked most about my boss Mike Boyle, the regional vice president of Fujitsu Business Communication Systems and an ex-Green Beret, is that he let me sink or swim.

He placed me in charge of one of the sixteen business units of this $150 million subsidiary of Fujitsu Limited. We sold voice, data, and video communications systems. I saw Mike four times a year and was given autonomy to do what needed to be done.

Boyle knew that business is a numbers game. I knew sales is a numbers game. That is how you keep score. I was given ultimate accountability for the profit and loss performance of my regional unit.

Profit is tied to the game called selling. One of my favorite Warren Buffett sayings is: "Games are won by players who focus on the playing field–not by those whose eyes are glued to the scoreboard." Before I invented the concept of smooth selling I instinctively started practicing it at Fujitsu by focusing on my playing field.

Actually the score was easy to know, because when I took the helm we were number sixteen out of sixteen business units. On top of that, on my first day we lost the Ford account, which accounted for half of our annual revenue.

My strategy for finding new revenue emerged. We rebuilt the direct sales team and indirect sales channels, devised and executed new marketing plans, and enhanced our customer service and technical support efforts, all while managing a union-technician workforce.

Over a three-year period total sales grew by 157 percent through the implementation of a comprehensive sales and marketing plan and the recruitment of qualified sales talent. In smooth selling it is necessary to match the sales strategy with the right sales talent. Our plan of establishing three strategic channel sales relationships generated an indirect channel sales increase of 1769 percent in those three years.

But having the right strategy and talent is not enough to win the game. A next step in the playbook is to attack gross profit margins. We increased gross profit margins by 32 percent (9.5 points) through the implementation of a well-targeted sales plan and operating efficiency improvements. Creating a sales plan with the assess, design, and deploy steps is crucial to increasing margins.

Great margins lead to great profits, which is the result of great execution of the sales plan. A plan is just a plan until it is properly executed. Our execution led to improved scores: an annual profit increase of $616,383, while improving return-on-sales to 8.8 percent from a minus 7.8 percent. We achieved those scores through sales volume and mix improvements, the implementation of cost controls, and operating efficiency gains.

This success was a team effort; I did not accomplish this alone. Also it was not personal bravado that led us from number sixteen to number one in sales productivity per sales rep. The lesson learned was it was a four-part system that did it: assess, design, deploy, and execute. An ex-Green Beret made me accountable to get it done, but did not micromanage me on how to get it done.

The key to getting it done was the strategy. The next chapter describes how to come up with a strategy that leads to smooth selling.

CHAPTER 4

Strategy

This is an old joke and I tell it for a reason. Two farmers were talking about how hard it was to make money farming. One farmer said: "Every week I take hay bales into town and sell them for $1 a bale. I sell all my bales but I am losing money."

The other farmer was quick to reply. "Oh that's an easy problem to solve," he said. "You need to buy a bigger truck."

Just increasing revenue is not always the best strategy. A sales strategy is the operating plan for a company's sales team. The strategy allocates sales resources efficiently to drive selling costs down and revenues up. The overall purpose is to get the most ROI from the sales force.

The Eight Great Components of an Effective Sales Strategy

With smooth selling, sales strategy can be broken down into eight strategic components:

Strategic Component One: Target Markets and Customer Segmentation

A first course of action is to identify those groups of customers that are of the most value to the business. These are the groups that predictably buy more and at better prices (higher margins). Knowing this will help drive selling costs down and enable your company to focus its product and service development efforts.

Strategic Component Two: Buying Personas and Influences

Identify those individuals by function within an organization that are likely to influence a purchase decision for the company's products or services. This includes the four key buying-influence roles: (1) economic, (2) technical, (3) user, and (4) coach. Covering your bases by interacting with these four buying influences will increase the probability of making a sale and making the sale at higher margins.

Strategic Component Three: Channel Strategy

Should the channel strategy be direct, indirect, or digital? Channel strategy drives selling costs down, drives revenues up, and potentially extends the market reach of a company. A company must determine the sales channels that can reach the target markets and customers most effectively. Some of the factors to weigh:

- Direct versus indirect versus digital sales team
- Hunter versus farmer sales team
- Inside versus outside sales team
- Complex solution versus transactional sales environment
- Salary heavy versus incentive heavy compensation plans
- Customized versus packaged products/services

Strategic Component Four: Sales/Customer Buying Process

In simple terms, a sales process is a systematic approach (a repeatable process) involving a series of steps that enables a sales force to close more deals, faster. The series of steps are customer-centric and help the sales force of a company to acquire new customers, retain current customers, and increase sales transaction volume as well as revenues. There are many reasons why this is important. Process increases lead conversion rates, shortens the sales cycle, increases the average dollar sale, improves profit margins, increases the productivity of the sales force, and drives selling costs down.

Strategic Component Five: Sales Message and Your Value Proposition

Your sales message is the unique message that the sales force delivers to target customers. This message is what sets your company apart from your competition. The message should be simple, presented from your customer's point-of-view, as well as memorable, and differentiating. Effectively communicating your company's uniqueness/value increases conversion rates, shortens the sales cycle, eliminates the competition, increases the average dollar sale, improves profit margins, and increases the productivity of your sales team.

Strategic Component Six: 5 x 5 Revenue Growth Strategies

Like any good investment portfolio, a business needs to diversify its sales growth investments. The five ways that any business can increase its revenues and gross profits are to:

- increase the number of sales leads coming into the business;
- improve the lead-to-close conversion rate;
- increase the number of annual customer transactions;
- increase the average dollar sale per transaction; and,
- improve gross profit margins.

By increasing performance by just 10 percent in each of these five areas, a business will increase revenues by 46 percent and gross profits by a massive 61 percent. It pays to do the math.

Strategic Component Seven: Performance Metrics

Performance metrics are the quantitative and qualitative measurements a business uses to measure the success or failure of its sales operations. These metrics should include both results- and activity-based measurements. What gets measured gets done, as the old adage goes. Performance metrics ensure that a business is using its sales resources efficiently to drive selling costs down and revenues up. Performance metric systems are discussed in detail in the following chapter.

Strategic Component Eight: Sales Compensation

Proper sales compensation ensures that a business can recruit and retain the most qualified sales talent as well as drive the desired sales behavior expected from members of the sales team. Five methods should be considered when a business decides how it will financially compensate the members of the sales team for their role in generating sales:

- Salary only
- Commission only
- Salary plus commission
- Salary plus bonus
- Spiffs

To do this right requires an assessment by an accomplished sales leader due to the number of variables involved. Done incorrectly, there will be unintended consequences.

The Octel Story

There is an old saying that it is easier to build an airplane from scratch than to rebuild an airplane while it is in the air. You don't always have the luxury of starting with a clean slate, but when you do it can be sweet.

My longest and most enjoyable tenure was when I started a regional operation from scratch at Octel Network Services (a.k.a. Ameritech Voice Messaging & Tigon Corporation). I was the regional vice president and reported to Freddie Carroll, the vice president of sales, who interestingly was an engineer by training.

Octel provided hosted voice messaging services for large corporations, public and private institutions, and government agencies. My job was to establish and direct the company's sales and customer support operations in twelve Midwest states.

This was the first time I was able to build a team from scratch. This was a new company, a new product, and there was no sales infrastructure at all.

What Carroll and I shared was a love of numbers. Over a seven-year period I was able to grow revenue from $0 to $16 million, a compounded annual revenue-growth rate (CAGR) of 54 percent, which are some lovable numbers. Revenue results are great, but never forget the three aspects that get you there: strategy, systems, and people.

The first aspect of strategy we looked at was who we should be targeting as prospects. Not all prospects are created alike. Which prospects offer you the best path to success and afford the least path of resistance? Once we identified our targets, then we identified the buying influencers.

Knowing the who helped us determine the what. Namely, what message to communicate that would catch the prospects in the heart. The message worked. This led me to sell and manage five of the company's top ten accounts: Inland Steel, Kraft Foods, Bank One, Ameritech, and the State of Wisconsin.

Overall, my sales team was recognized as the top sales region in six of the seven years. However, strategy alone did not produce those top sales results. What did get us there was a sales system, a repeatable sales process that consistently produced results. Creating such a system is the focus of the next chapter.

CHAPTER 5

Systems

One of the foundations of smooth selling forever is the concept of sales enablement. Indeed, sales enablement is necessary for every step of the buying cycle and works to optimize all interactions with potential buyers.

Forrester Research defines sales enablement as "a strategic, ongoing process that equips all client-facing employees with the ability to consistently and systematically have a valuable conversation with the right set of customer stakeholders at each stage of the customer's problem-solving life cycle to optimize the return on investment in the selling system."

To achieve smooth selling a company must align sales and marketing efforts to improve sales performance. In brief, the goal is sales optimization. In my experience this means seeking to optimize systems in eight areas.

The Eight Great Sales Enablement Systems

An America's Cup team is highly selective about which sailors are allowed to crew the ship. A company should be equally selective about who sells its products or services. Once your smooth selling crew is aboard, then you need to do everything you can to enable them to sell.

System One: Hiring

Hiring is too important to leave to a seat-of-the-pants approach. A hiring process should employ a series of time-tested steps. A person within the organization should be assigned responsibility for each step and a timeframe followed. Here is a seventeen-step recommendation:

- Complete a job role worksheet
- Develop position description
- Develop recruitment ad
- Develop candidate-screening questionnaire
- Develop on-boarding plan
- Place recruitment ad
- Screen resumes received

- Screen resume qualified candidates using candidate-screening questionnaire
- Select top candidates using their resume, answers to the candidate-screening questionnaire and available social media information
- Conduct telephone interviews with all qualified candidates
- Conduct initial face-to-face interviews with all qualified candidates
- Conduct reference checks on candidates moving to next round interviews
- Complete a psychometric sales assessment on candidates moving to next round interviews
- Conduct team member interviews with all qualified candidates
- Conduct final interview top two candidates
- Extend job offer in writing
- Conduct background check

During the process the hiring company needs to determine its expectations for success for the sales person. These are important to communicate and should guide the sales-candidate filtering process. Some questions to ask include:

- Describe your experience selling (insert the products or services that the company sells).
- What types of organizations have you been selling to over the past three years?
- By role, who was involved in the buying decision and who was the primary decision maker?
- What was your average deal size in each of the past three years?
- What was the monthly dollar value of your average sales pipeline and how many prospects were included in it in each of the past three years?
- How long was your average sales cycle and how many face-to-face sales calls were typically required to close a sale in each of the past three years?
- What level of quota attainment did you achieve and what was your performance rank versus your peers in each of the past three years?

- Over the course of your sales career what formal sales training have you received and when?
- What has been your earning history, breaking apart salary from incentive compensation, over the past three years?

After an interview, each candidate should be evaluated based on a predetermined set of success characteristics. Every company is different so weight should be given to each characteristic (is it critical, a plus, or a basic need?). My suggestion is simple scoring on a 0 to 3 scale (3 = exceeds expectations, 2 = meets expectations, 1 = short of expectations, and 0 = lacks the characteristic). Here are some characteristics to examine:

- Industry sales experience
- Understanding of the sales environment
- Sales track record
- Sales cycle fit
- Sales transaction size fit
- Formal sales training
- Income fit
- Personality/cultural fit

If your company plans to use an outside recruiter the steps will remain virtually the same, however in addition to finding qualified candidates, your recruiter should also be held accountable for prescreening candidates and presenting only candidates that meet your selection criteria.

System Two: Training

Onboarding (new hire training) is as important as hiring right. A company should develop a checklist of onboarding steps for new sales people. In addition to basic HR items like company orientation, payroll, and computer access, there needs to be sales specific steps. These include to name a few:

- Introduction to a peer mentor
- Role training
- Role training quiz
- Product and pricing training
- Product and pricing quiz
- Marketing and messaging training
- Marketing and messaging quiz
- Competition and differentiation training

- Competition and differentiation quiz
- Differentiation roleplay
- Sales process training
- Sales support systems training
- Sales process and support systems quiz
- Communication tools training
- Lead management training
- Lead management quiz
- Shadowing a great example
- Mock sales call training
- RFP submission training
- Mock RFP submission and review

In addition to initial training, ongoing weekly coaching and mentoring is critical to ensuring long-term sales success.

System Three: Sales/Buying Process

A defined and documented sales/buying process gives a company a game plan or in nautical terms, a map for making sales. The process also gives the organization a common language to discuss the status of a potential deal, the probability of making a sale, and where a breakdown might be occurring. Here is a sample of what a sales/buying process might look like in the simplest of terms:

- Stage 1: Suspect Identified
- Stage 2: Suspect Pre-qualified
- Stage 3: Prospect Needs Assessment Completed
- Stage 4: Proposal Presented
- Stage 5: Contract Submitted
- Stage 6: Verbal Agreement Received
- Stage 7: Sale Won, Written Agreement Received
- Stage 8: Sale Lost
- Stage 9: Sale Abandoned by Prospect
- Stage 10: Sale Abandoned by Company

System Four: Goal Setting and Budgeting

Goal setting and budgeting require serious conversations and then memorializing the results of those conversations in writing. A company should have standardized worksheets for documenting goals and action plans for the year. Once a goal is determined, then begins the process of thinking backward to determine the necessary action steps required to reach the goal.

Setting quotas and expense budgets requires constructing a mathematical formula based on several variables. These variables include:

- Target revenue
- Average deal size
- Number of deals needed
- Opportunity-to-close ratio
- Total opportunities required
- Hours needed by rep per lead generated
- Total hours of work per rep for lead follow up
- Total hours needed to close an opportunity
- Length of time to close an opportunity
- Rep productivity percentage
- Selling hours available per rep
- Closed deals per rep
- Fully loaded cost per rep

Time assumptions also must be figured into the equation. These include non-work days in a year, vacation/sick/holidays in a year, total work days, hours per day, hours per year. Like a complicated word problem from math class, the quota setting process reveals how many reps are required to reach the desired revenue, the quota needed per rep, and how much it will cost the company to obtain the desired revenue.

Once quotas are assigned, then the sales activity necessary to achieve the assigned quotas can be calculated using simple math. This helps a company know what its numbers should be on a daily (based on 240 work days), weekly (based on 48 work weeks), monthly, quarterly, and annual basis. The elements of these calculations include:

- Assigned quota
- Average revenue per sale
- Opportunity-to-close ratio
- Number of sales calls required to close a sale
- Number of prospecting calls needed to identify an opportunity
- Average opportunities per account

System Five: Forecasting

Another area that needs mathematical rigor is forecasting. Sloppy inputs will produce sloppy results.

There is a sales axiom that not all prospects are created equal. To determine who best to focus resources on, begin with a targeting analysis of ideal customers. My recommendation is to start the exercise with the sales team by identifying your top twenty prospective deals by customer. This is not educated guesswork. Again, rigor is required. The objective is to determine potential spend by product or solution sets. Do this by performing the following steps:

- Append your existing customer data with the appropriate third-party data
- Determine the variables that best predict the spend with your company
- Define the weighting and scoring for each correlated variable to calculate potential
- Compare calculated potential with actual spending to determine cross sell and upsell potential
- Apply weighting and scoring from step three

to the prospects that look most like your best customers.

Another aspect of forecasting is evaluating opportunities. This is done on an account-by-account basis. What you are looking to determine is which of the four stages a prospect is in and where the company stands. The first stage looks to see if the buyer is motivated to investigate other options. The second stage is about the buyer identifying needs. The third stage is about the prospect evaluating options. The fourth stage is about the buyer selecting a solution, and will your company win the opportunity. Each stage can be analyzed by asking a series of questions.

Stage one: Questions to determine the strength of the opportunity

- Are we at the right time in the buyer's process?
- Are they willing to provide the information we need to do good discovery?
- Is there a compelling event that is important enough for the prospect to take action?
- Have we clearly established the buyer's expressed needs?

- Has the buyer explored this challenge or need before?
- Has the buyer established a timeframe for addressing the need?
- Has the buyer budgeted money to pay for a solution?

Stage two: Questions to determine if the buyer is aware of the need

- Does the buyer have a vision of the solution?
- Has the buyer offered staff time to assist with the discovery?
- Do we have access to the right technical and business info?
- Do we have the ability to shape the buyer's vision?

Stage three: Questions to determine if the buyer is actively evaluating options

- Has the buyer seen your product or service in action?
- Do we have unique differentiators from the buyer's point-of-view?
- Are we well positioned in the industry from this buyer's point-of-view?

- Does the final approver have a high priority pain?
- Do we have access to all of the buying influencers?
- Do all of the buying influencers believe we have a differentiated vision?
- Has the final approver accepted our business case and ROI?
- Do we have a coach who wants us to win?

Stage four: Questions to determine if the buyer is selecting a solution

- Do we have a strong relationship with all the key buying influencers?
- Do we have regular access to the final approver?
- Do we have a superior relationship with all the key buying influencers versus the competition?
- Do we have evidence that we have significantly lowered the buyer's resistance to change?

See how many yes answers you get at each stage. If a company cannot muster enough yes answers, then it really cannot proceed to the next stage. The good news, or hard truth, is critical for forecasting future sales.

System Six: Performance Metrics

In sales, performance metrics are about keeping score as the game is on. For a moment, let's depart from the metaphor of sailing. That is a race and it is easy to tell if you are winning or losing a race. Imagine instead a sport like baseball or football, and the importance of the scoreboard.

A good sales scorecard provides a readout of all the key activity- and results-based metrics required to achieve predictable and sustainable success, both on an individual and team roll-up basis. This is a published look at targets and average performance on a week-by-week basis. Some of the metrics on the scorecard to include are:

- New Opportunities (new and existing accounts; number and dollar value)
- Sales Meetings (prospect first time, prospect follow-on, existing accounts)
- Proposals Delivered (new and existing accounts; number and dollar value)

- Active Opportunity Pipeline (total dollar value, number of opportunities, and average dollar value per opportunity)
- Orders Booked (new and existing accounts; number and dollar value)
- Won-Loss-No Decisions (new and existing accounts; number and dollar value)
- Quota Performance (new and existing accounts; percentage and dollar value achievement against assigned quotas)

System Seven: Performance Evaluation

Performance planning and assessment should be done on a regular basis. When done right, this is a communication tool that is a key part of sales enablement. Elements of a written planning and assessment template should include the following:

- Role mandate, based on business objectives and priorities
- Key accountabilities and accomplishments
- Performance objectives and accomplishments
- Personal effectiveness delivering results and working collaboratively

- Development objectives to improve skills and knowledge
- Overall summary of contributions
- Performance rating (exceptional, successful, below expectations)

So what do you do if the contribution is below expectations? Use a Performance Improvement Plan (PIP) when you have identified employee performance problems. The PIP plays an integral role in correcting performance discrepancies. It is a tool to monitor and measure unacceptable performance against the scorecard. In constructing a PIP, follow the guidelines below:

- Define the problem using *deficiency statements* and always tie it back to the published scorecard. These clearly define the problems that exist with the performance and/or behavior of the employee. Each deficiency should be identified in a separate statement and should be directly related. For example: "Employee fails to complete assignments in a timely manner." Such statements should be supported by appropriate documentation.

- Determine if the problem is an *accountabilities problem* (employee has not been able to get the job done) or a *competencies problem* (employee does not perform the job the right way).
- Define the *accountabilities* where improvement is required and indicate what aspects of performance are required to successfully perform these accountabilities.
- Define the *competencies* where improvement is required and indicate what aspects of performance are required to successfully perform these competencies.

- Establish the *priorities* of the duties.
  - What are the possible consequences of errors associated with these duties?
  - How frequently are these duties performed?
  - How do they relate when compared with other duties?

- Establish *goals and timetables* for accomplishing change in performance/behavior.

- Develop an *action plan.*
  - What will the manager do to help the employee accomplish the goals?

- What will the employee do to facilitate improvement of the product or process?
- Are the items reasonable?
- Can the items be accomplished?
- Are the items flexible?

- Define *measurement cadence.*
  - Establish periodic review dates (weekly to monthly)
  - Measure actual performance against the standards

- Establish a Performance Improvement Plan *file* for the employee. Check the *wording* to see that you:
  - Use plain and simple language
  - Cite specific references to identify areas of deficiency

Last step. Sign it along with the employee.

System Eight: Technology

A customer relationship management (CRM) system can improve a company's relationship with existing customers, as well as facilitate its quest to secure new prospective customers, and win back former customers.

One of the prime benefits of using a CRM system, customized to support your business needs, is enhancing customer satisfaction. By using this tool, all dealings involving servicing, marketing, and selling your products or services to customers can be carried out (and documented) in an organized and systematic way. Using the data collected, a company can improve the effectiveness of marketing campaigns and improve sales efficiency. A CRM system also facilitates upselling and cross selling.

Here are some questions to ask when assessing CRM needs:

- How many initial and potential CRM users do you envision having in your organization, categorized by role (management, sales/marketing, customer service, and administration)?
- For what purposes will your sales and support teams be expected to use their computers?
- What hardware is in use today (desktop computers, laptops, tables, smart phones, and servers)?
- How old is the hardware you are using today?

- What software do you use? (Outlook? Accounting? Sales database?)
- Do you or will you do written proposals and quotes? How do you track them?
- How do you generate leads? How do you track them?
- What do you do for marketing and what is the budget (direct mail, website, SEO, pay-per-click, advertising, trade shows, gifts, trips, etc.)?

Roy Chomko's Story

In 2001, Roy Chomko co-founded Adage Technologies, combining a passion for technology and the desire to build a company focused on driving business value through web technology. As president, Chomko's energy and customer-centric approach have helped to grow Adage into a well-respected, award-winning creator of content-rich websites and e-commerce solutions.

But like any business, there were challenges. Chomko was stretched thin and needed a better sales infrastructure. He knew he needed to change if he was to continue growing fast. Chomko was a rugby player and he knew you won rugby matches by getting the fundamentals right.

As a sales consultant, I helped him install a complete new sales infrastructure. We put sales processes in place, along with performance metrics, a goal and quota-setting system, a structured forecasting process, a hiring system, a format for facilitating productive group and one-to-one sales meetings, and customized his CRM system for activity tracking and performance reporting purposes.

Here is what a smooth selling system and accountability can do in a short time. Adage increased booked orders by 32 percent, forecasted sales by 142 percent and the sales pipeline by 26 percent during the first nine months of working together. Year over year sales increased by 51 percent.

Sales enablement systems enhance the ability of the sales team to increase company revenue through smooth selling. But it takes organized sales people performing at their best to make it all work. How to make that organized effort happen on a systematic and consistent basis is examined at depth in the next chapter.

Chapter 6

People

Winning skippers of the America's Cup will always credit their crew. Indeed, the racing syndicates know that technology will only take them so far. Strategy in sailing is critical, but it is not everything. Success also depends on the proper handling of the craft and the correct execution of the strategy.

Bob Oliver's Story

Bob Oliver, president at Lucent Public Safety Systems in Lisle, Illinois, came to appreciate the importance of organizing people. Oliver was a Northwestern grad who became a career senior-level corporate executive. He was tasked with dressing the company up for sale, but the prospects looked bleak.

Oliver brought me in as vice president of sales and marketing. Immediately it became apparent that the challenge at the company was that everybody in sales was trying to sell everything to anybody. As a result, nobody was buying.

The company had multiple product lines that were being sold to entirely different markets. Some products were sold to telephone companies and other products to 911 public-safety answering points (think police departments). Those are entirely different markets that require different selling processes and different types of sales people. As a result the sales people, to quote an old saying, were trying to be jacks of all trades and were masters of none. That is the opposite of setting your sales people up for success.

So we reorganized the company sales department from being a product-centric to a customer-centric one. Which meant sales reps who understood police departments sold market-specific products to those markets and sales people who understood telephone companies sold products to those markets.

The reorganization of the sales department allowed us to develop a deeper understanding of customer needs, which generated increased sales and reduced costs. This also increased the "stickiness" around customer relationships. Furthermore, it allowed us to take a customer-centric approach to our product development efforts, as opposed to our former product-push approach.

People made the difference because we were able to get the right sales people aligned with the right customers. Instead of one sales team we decided we needed three.

In smooth selling nautical terms, different type boats are needed for different type races. And different types of boats require different crews. (In horse racing parlance, the phrase is "different horses for different courses.")

What were the results? We launched an $8 million call center business. In the two years the company was up for sale we achieved 108 percent and 113 percent of sales plan and I personally secured a professional services contract with a Fortune 100 company valued at $21.3 million over three years.

Eight Great Ways to Organize Sales People

Regardless of which way is best for the company, there are eight great ways to organize the sales people to ensure smooth selling.

People One: Structure/Organizational Design

This point is repeated for emphasis: alas, people need to be set up for success. This begins with a five-step territory design approach.

- **Analyze Potential**. Use existing customer data to determine how much they currently spend. Then, to determine account level potential, apply the current spend to customer and prospect data.
- **Rank Sales People**. Begin by determining the current territory potential. Next determine how much revenue the sales rep should be able to attain. This allows you to determine the potential percentage penetration for each rep and territory. Finally, rank the sales people by the potential penetration percentages.
- **Map Prospects and Customers to Territories**. This is both science and art. Several factors go into the mapping process: account location based on headquarters location, account potential based on the current spend analysis, preferred industries, enterprise or business unit revenue cutoff, and account workload of the sales rep.

- **Produce Territories**. Each territory takes into account the following: prospect potential, customer potential, workload required, number of prospect accounts, and number of customer accounts.
- **Review Territory Map.** This is the opportunity to fine tune. Look at sales rep ranking vs. the potential of the territory and see if any moves are required. Then look at the list of the accounts the sales rep has and decide if you need to add or subtract. Look at the existing pipeline of the sales rep and the number and value of deals potentially taking place. Based on that make final adjustments and re-run the territory map.

Like any complicated endeavor, from flying airplanes to performing surgery, a checklist approach for smooth selling is most helpful. Here is the method to take stock and make sure no aspect is being overlooked. Your master checklist should include these major categories:

- **Segmentation**. Items include: competitor analysis, ideal customer profile, account potential, customer-acquisition cost, life-time value, propensity to buy, and buyer process maps.

- **Planning**. Items include pro-forma revenue/cost model, revenue key performance indicators, sales plan, resource allocation, budget method, approved budget, approved headcount, data architecture, data cleanliness, and data stewardship.
- **Engagement**. Items include: social selling, prospecting, sales process, adoption, field testing, and sales-manager coaching.
- **Organization**. Items include: buyer channel preference, channel coverage, competitive channel analysis, org chart stress testing, time study, talent assessment, candidate selection, new hire onboarding, performance setting, territory design, quota setting, and compensation plans.
- **Execution.** Items include: content audit, sales training, technology automation, adoption plan, pipeline management, forecast management, and data/analytics/reporting strategy.
- **Support**. Items include: pricing exceptions, contract exceptions, comp exceptions, marketing automation, CRM, partner resource

management, contract administration, configure/price/quote, quote-to-revenue, and online collaboration.

People Two: Defined Roles and Responsibilities

What do your sales people expect from you? Do you clearly understand what you expect of them? Conversations about expectations don't count if that is all you do. As the movie mogul Samuel Goldwyn was alleged to have said, "An oral agreement isn't worth the paper it is written on." Expectations need to be in writing. List responsibilities, authority, and performance metrics.

People Three: Staffing and Hiring Plans

Arguably nothing is more important than getting the right people on the team. When you talk about finding the right person, you are talking about the right person for the right job. Many companies rush the process and regret that they hired in haste. Here is a checklist approach to follow:

- Complete a job role worksheet
- Develop position description
- Develop recruitment ad
- Develop candidate screening questionnaire

- Develop on-boarding plan
- Place recruitment ad
- Screen resumes received
- Screen resume qualified candidates using candidate screening questionnaire
- Select top candidates using their resume, answers to the candidate screening questionnaire and available social media information
- Conduct telephone interviews with all qualified candidates
- Conduct initial face-to-face interviews with all qualified candidates
- Conduct reference checks on candidates moving to next round interviews
- Complete a psychometric sales assessment on candidates moving to next round interviews
- Conduct team member interviews with all qualified candidates
- Conduct final interview top two candidates
- Extend job offer in writing
- Conduct background check

Each of the items on this list could be a full chapter in a book. Allow me to expound on just a few.

The position description is a simple document that requires some serious thinking. In addition to position summary, thought needs to be given to key responsibilities and measures of effectiveness. Next comes a list of the necessary skills and attributes the company is seeking, which includes: academic, experience, computer skills, communications skills, attitudes, and behavior.

A posting template is a communication tool to help candidates determine if they should apply and be considered for the position. The goal is as much up-front clarity as possible. This document explains the role profile, the role purpose, compensation and benefits, potential territory, reporting structure, why they should want the job, what they will be doing, preferred qualifications and experience, top preferred competencies, desired skills, the sales culture, how they will be measured, and the hiring process.

The expectations written in the position description and posting template lead to the creation of the sales candidate filtering questions. This helps the interviewer probe for proper fit. It is fair game to discuss average deal size, average monthly pipeline value, sales cycles, quota attainment, and compensation packages.

A final note: top sales candidates are wooed by many companies throughout their career. While a company is screening candidates, candidates are likewise screening companies. How a company handles the process sends important clues on what it will be like to work for that company. A process that is less than top notch is a hindrance to attracting top talent.

People Four: Personnel Assessment

Systems for performance evaluation were discussed in the previous chapter. From a people perspective there are some finer points to be considered.

Individuals are to be evaluated against certain Key Performance Measures that are essential for effective performance. For example, the language might read:

> *Our Company has selected two Key Performance Measures applicable to all people throughout the organization. These measures under the heading of "Critical Company Competencies" are:*

- *Alignment with Business Objectives*
- *Client Focus and Quality of Service*

Ah, performance ratings. One of the most misunderstood parts of evaluation is the application of performance ratings. Many managers are guilty of performance-rating inflation. The individual's performance on each of the key performance measures and his or her overall job performance should be evaluated on the basis of the following ratings:

5 - Exceptional Performance. Performance consistently and significantly exceeds expectations and requirements on the job. An individual at this level demonstrates outstanding proficiency in performing unique or critical tasks and/or difficult or complex aspects of the job competently and thoroughly. Quality and quantity of work is excellent and creative or new applications are made regularly.

4 - Exceeds Expectations. Performance exceeds requirements in a number of key areas. A high level of skill is demonstrated. Contributions are significant. Performance adds value beyond what is expected.

3 - Meets Expectations. Performance is solid, meets required standards and expectations, and is what is expected of a fully competent and qualified person in the position. An individual at this level consistently contributes to the success of the work group.

2 - Improvement Needed. Performance is slightly below acceptable levels, occasionally fails to meet the minimum standards of job performance, or is poor/inconsistent. Immediate improvement is needed; however with guidance and training, this may be achieved. Disciplinary or corrective action may be needed if performance does not progress to "meets expectations".

1 – Unsatisfactory. Performance does not meet expectations and is unacceptable. An individual at this level requires more assistance, supervision, and follow-up than is acceptable on a continuing basis. Significant and immediate improvement is needed. An overall rating of "unsatisfactory" requires disciplinary or corrective action.

A *performance summary section* is used to assess the individual's overall performance during the entire review period. This is done by adding the numerical ratings of the objectives and key performance measures and then dividing the total ratings by the number of objectives and key performance measures to arrive at an overall average rating.

A *performance objectives and development plans section* is used to document major accountabilities and objectives for the next review period and the corresponding action or development plans to accomplish the stated objectives. This section is to be finalized after the individual and supervisor have agreed upon desired areas of improvement and development needs relating to upcoming goals.

People Five: Sales Training Programs

Onboarding was discussed in the previous chapter. In this chapter on people the attention turns to ongoing training.

Why does a successful America's Cup team train and train and train. The crews know how to sail. And yet, they practice over and over again. Why? The answer is obvious and makes a good analogy. Because the race is so important they want to be as prepared as possible to win. Experienced skippers know too that crews require coaching to reach top performance.

Likewise, much is at stake when a sales rep is in front of the prospect or the customer. To achieve top sales performance it is imperative to engage in ongoing coaching. The objective of the sales leader should be to improve the major interactions of the sales reps on the team. The sales leader can use the following questions to coach with an objective of improving performance:

1. Where is the buyer in their process?
2. What are your objectives for the call? How will you measure success?
3. What is the customer's desired outcome?
4. Who will be present from the customer? (Name, title, buying role, level of influence)
5. What questions is each persona/stakeholder asking that you need to answer in this call to progress the deal?
6. What story are you telling? Will it drive action?
7. What resistance will you face?

8. How do you plan to engage the audience?
9. What insight are you going to provide that will differentiate you from other sales people that call on this customer?
10. Who is attending the meeting from our side? What will their role be? Have you fully prepared them?
11. What is the desired next step?

People Six: Leadership Development

In America's Cup racing, just because someone is a great sailor does not necessarily mean that they will make a great skipper. This is similar to the sales adage that "A great sales person doesn't always a great sales leader make."

Before someone is made a sales leader their competency should be tested. Here are five areas that need to be examined.

- **Selling Skills**. This can encompass nearly two dozen facets. These include command of sales approach, handling objections, prospecting, lead management, technology proficiency, and content production.

- **Management Skills**. There are probably a dozen management skills a sales leader should have at their disposal. These include team building, managing diversity, resourcefulness, and conflict management.
- **Communications Skills**. Good leaders need to be good communicators. That doesn't mean good talkers. These include active listening, presentation skills, written communications, oral communications, and abstract reasoning.
- **Intellectual Capacity**. Great leaders are smart. But there is more than one kind of smarts. Common sense and street smarts are to be prized. There are about a half-dozen intellectual areas that are important. These include intelligence, innovation, creativity, judgment, and pragmatism.
- **Interpersonal Skills**. Being personable is great, but it is not enough. There are more than a dozen areas of importance when it comes to interpersonal skills. These include passion, ambition, tenacity, work/life balance, flexibility, persuasion, assertiveness, and energy.

Sales leaders are made, not born. In other words, no one is perfect and all must be developed. Newly promoted sales managers should be developed in a number of areas. These include strategy and customer management, process and productivity, sales talent management, and use of metrics and rewards. School is never out for the sales leader; there is always something new to be learned and improved upon.

People Seven: Sales Leader Recruitment

The quality of your sales leader recruitment process will help get the best leadership on your sales team. This one item will allow you to recruit sales people and leaders inside or outside the industry. You will get the best sales person and sales leader for the role this way. A great hiring process has defined accountabilities and competences for the role. It includes a phone screen, work interview, competency interviews and a job tryout.

Having a sales process that is mapped to your customers buying process is key. This will eliminate the need for industry-only sales people as you have documented the way your customers buy. Providing this process, along with some basic product training, will enable you to hire the best sales person for the position and not just the best in your industry.

Certifying sales managers means you have training curriculum. This training must include courses on situational leadership and coaching/ developing sales people. By not having this training, your newly hired sales people have to rely on self-critique to improve. This signifies the need for an industry-only hire.

Focusing your sales managers on coaching and developing allows the product knowledge a non-industry sales person doesn't have to improve. But more importantly the problems your product or service solves can be understood quickly by the non-industry person. The industry sales person will also benefit greatly from this coaching and developing.

Segmentation is a key part of a great sales strategy. This allows you to point any sales person to the best opportunities inside their territories. Good segmentation allows you to hire a non-industry sales person if you want. But without it, you almost have to hire an industry sales person. They will know inside a territory where those best accounts or prospects are. Otherwise, you have to tell them.

People Eight: Compensation

There is a great adage in sales: "What gets rewarded gets done." Many worthy books and articles have been written on the subject. In the interest of brevity, the following is what I have gleaned through my years in sales. Here are fifteen best practices when it comes to reviewing an organization's sales plan.

- Review the plan for effectiveness more than once per year. Is it driving the behaviors you have defined as critical?
- The plan includes an account loss-mitigation provision. What's the procedure in the event a large existing client is lost?
- There exists a compensation communication plan which provides details frequently and transparently to the team. Where do reps and managers go when they have questions?
- The impact of the plan is assessed against existing individual sales people and managers. Has the plan been modeled using actual employees' existing performance to evaluate the before and after effects?

- The plan is not based on optimistic forecasts. Are the forecasts and quota assumptions used in the plan believable? Or aspirational?
- The plan was piloted in a controlled setting prior to roll out.
- The comp plan does not cap compensation. There is a defined method of accounting for unusual circumstances, monster deals, etc., but in general compensation should not be capped.
- The comp plan is matched to your business lifecycle.
- The incentive portion of the plan contains no more than three metrics.
- No single incentive metric accounts for less than 15 percent of the total available incentive compensation.
- Quotas are not cookie-cutter, but are based on the total available market for each territory.
- There is a defined process and set of criteria to request exceptions to the plan.
- You've tested the comp plan against your

industry. How do your industry competitors pay compared to you?

- You've tested the comp plan against your talent competitors. You don't just compete for sales talent in your own industry – you compete in the larger market as well. Sites like glassdoor.com can be a starting point.
- Your existing technology is sufficient to manage the plan. Are different parts of the organization using different methods or tools to calculate payouts?

Final Thoughts on People

What can a company do to set its sales people up for success? Providing qualified leads to your sales people increases their win rate, average sales price and decreases average sales cycle length. Non-industry-hired sales people will benefit from these leads and close them typically faster than industry-hired sales people. A lead management process helps make the non-industry sales person ramp quicker and faster allowing you to choose the best sales person and not be limited to industry sales people only.

Product training is also key and a necessity to hiring any sales person. But it is more important with non-industry sales people. You have to train your sales people on your products or services to be successful.

Farming existing accounts for retention and cross-sell/upsell opportunities is more favorable to hiring sales people from your industry. Knowing the products will help your customers get value from the farmer sooner and more often. However, if you primarily hunt or have low account penetration, hiring from outside the industry would work better as this requires selling skills that can be used in any industry.

SECTION III

Sales Plan Execution Now and Forever

"My goal in sailing isn't to be brilliant or flashy in individual races, just to be consistent over the long run."

—DENNIS CONNER, FOUR-TIME AMERICA'S CUP WINNING SKIPPER

There is more to smooth selling than just enhancing the ability of the sales team to increase company revenue by closing more deals. A real test for a company is not doing it for a single concerted effort, but to achieve smooth selling consistently for the long race ahead.

Chapter 7

Staying on Course

There is no *set it and forget it* when it comes to smooth selling. Putting together a smooth selling system takes a great deal of work, but it is not the only work that needs to be done from a strategic standpoint. Sales processes, performance metrics, performance reviews, staffing plans, and more need to be reviewed on a regular basis.

An analogy can be drawn once again from the world of competitive sailing. The term smooth sailing, which means easy progress, is an idiom that alludes to calm waters. The phrase, which brings to mind sailing vessels free from big waves or roughness, has been in usage dating from the late 1300s.

However, in sailing like in selling, this is not always the case. While it would be great to have the wind at your back and to proceed through calm waters ahead, often more is required to reach your destination successfully. Oftentimes a vessel must sail into the wind.

Sailors well know that sailing maneuvers like tacking are required when you must sail into the wind. Tacking, or coming about, is an adjustment by which a sailing vessel turns its bow into wind so that the direction from which the wind blows changes from one side to the other. Tacking allows the sailing ship to make progress in a zig-zag or saw-tooth-type pattern.

The best strategy is to change course when the situation requires, and to stay on a favorable tack as much as possible. That produces nautical inertia that propels a ship through the waves. Skippers also want to shorten the time on an unfavorable tack, which results in faster passage with less wasted effort.

If while on a tack the wind shifts in the favor of the sailing vessel, that is called a lift and it creates a tack that is even more favorable. But if the wind shifts against the vessel, then the opposite tack may become the more favorable course. That is why the skipper must monitor the conditions and change course when needed for the most efficient passage.

This is an apt metaphor for the smooth selling system. There needs to be a watchful skipper at the helm deciding when to maneuver and adjust. This allows an organization to take a favorable course and tack when that is necessary.

Checklist to Stay on Course with Smooth Selling

The right amount of time to monitor your entire smooth selling system is on a quarterly basis. Monthly is too frequent and can hurt inertia if too much tinkering takes place. However, semi-annually is allowing too much time to transpire before a necessary adjustment is made. Four times a year is the perfect rhythm for the monitoring and adjustment.

To monitor the smooth selling system, use this checklist in your quarterly reviews.

1. **Is the detailed sales plan understood by the entire sales team?**

   An organization must know where it wants to go and when it wants to get there. A written list should be created with targeted accounts and the corresponding decision makers. The list must include clear deadlines and accountability for reaching the goal. This is clearly stated in writing.

2. **Does the sales message differentiate your company from the competition?**
   There are three musts: the message must be simple, the message must be from the customer's point-of-view, and the message must be memorable.

3. **Does the compensation plan incent desired behavior?**
   What gets rewarded gets done. The comp plan should provide the right incentives. A correct comp plan is a win-win for the sales rep and the organization. The right comp plans should help attract the right salespeople.

4. **Is the defined sales process clearly understood and executable?**
   Each step of the sales process must be clearly stated. This creates a common language and understanding of sales success. The important aspect is to define checkpoints for each step in the sales process.

5. **Are the sales metrics clearly defined?**
   Attention must be paid to how a company is keeping score of sales activity. This is how a company sets the proper activity levels it

desires. This provides a common scorekeeping system for what is defined as good and bad. Furthermore, this is how to determine future success before it is too late.

6. **Is the sales team staffed properly?**
   The sales team must be led by a sales manager for top results. There needs to be a proper structure to maximize sales, such as outside versus inside reps and reps that are hunters versus reps that are farmers. Moreover, there needs to be the right number of the right people in each role on the team.

7. **Is the short-term and/or long-term sales pipeline and forecasting tool working?**
   A sales pipeline provides a bottom-up view because each sales rep can see what is being produced. This helps the sales manager align costs with expected revenue. Monitoring the pipeline is one of the most effective sales management tools for a sales manager.

8. **Is the customer relationship management (CRM) system running properly?**
   A first step is to determine the proper application of CRM for the team. CRM is not one size fits all, and should be customized to match

the company's sales processes and customer acquisition and support structure. This is the single repository for all sales activity. This is where multiple departments can see the status of sales activities and deal progression.

9. **Are annual performance reviews in place?**
   An annual performance review forces a manager to sit down and evaluate performance. This is the time to set goals for the following year. Then progress should be tracked and discussed on a quarterly basis. This also lays the foundation for performance improvement and, if necessary, termination.

10. **Is effective sales skills training and sales mentoring in place?**
    A sales leader should travel with sales reps to determine their competency. With that knowledge training can be customized to fit each rep's need. The best training is role playing to test a rep's ability to apply what he or she has been taught. Practice improves performance.

11. **Are sales meetings happening on a weekly basis?**
    Each member of a sales team should know what is expected of them each week. That is

why every member of the sales team should be included in a weekly meeting. The sales leader should make sure everyone comes prepared to report on their expected deliverables.

12. **Is an effective lead generation system in place?**

While sales reps should always be on the watch for good prospects, there should be a lead generation program in place to feed them qualified leads.

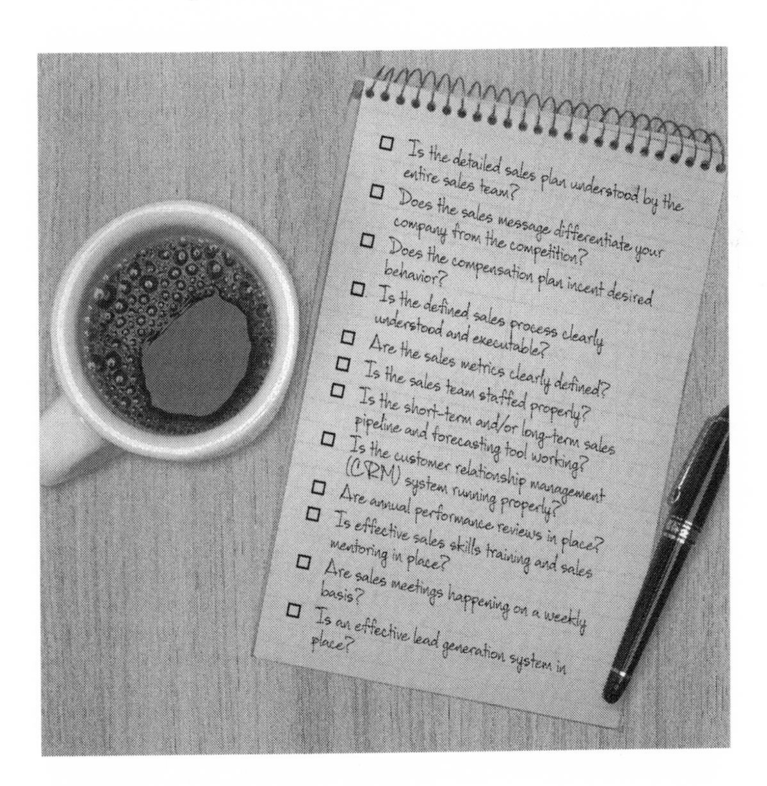

Jeff Robertson's Story

How do you win a battle against bigger, better known competitors? That was the challenge facing Jeff Robertson, a career public safety official and ex-police officer who was president and CEO of Tel Control, Inc. when he brought me on board as vice president of sales and marketing. Founded in 1969, Tel Control designs and manufactures systems that manage 911 emergency communications at the city, county, and state level.

My task was to participate in a company relaunch, lead the branding effort including the launch of a new product. As a result of the smooth selling system we put in place, the company was able to grow sales by 142 percent within the first six months and secure two multi-million-dollar strategic alliances.

In essence, this was a business restart. The situation was we had to introduce a new product that fit the needs of the market. The company was trying to do this with a direct sales organization competing against entrenched providers. That was a fight we could not win.

So instead of taking the competition head on with a herd of hunters, we tried a different sales tack. Rather than concentrate on direct sales, we changed the focus to selling through channels and building relationships with telephone companies and other 911 emergency communication system value-added resellers (VARs).

The first step in our strategy was to get mind share at these well-established telephone companies and VARs, and that calls for farmers. So we stocked our channel sales team with farmers willing to build and nurture relationships.

We put in a documented sales process, assigned quotas to make sure our revenue-generation plan would be covered, and made sure everyone understood the detailed sales plan. Each quarter we monitored progress to make sure we were on track.

The foundation of this strategy was recognizing that the telephone companies and VARs were already in front of the right prospects. Furthermore, they had the credibility we lacked. The number one job of our channel sales team was to prove to the telephone companies and VARS that going with us would be a safe decision.

Once we convinced the telephone companies and VARs of our 911 system's worth, we became a value-added offering they could propose to their government clients that needed phone systems and upgraded 911 system capability. This did more than just get our foot in the door. These add-on sales helped our channel partners, and it reduced the risk to the governmental public safety organizations because we were vetted by a well-established, bigger brand.

Once we acquired two multi-million-dollar strategic alliances, it truly was smooth selling ahead. However, we did not rest. We kept looking to the future, which is the topic of the next and final chapter.

Chapter 8

Keep Looking to the Horizon

There is a smooth selling forever lesson to be gleaned from the career of the greatest America's Cup skipper of all time.

From 1987 through to 2003, Dennis Conner was skipper of the celebrated Stars & Stripes yachts. His accomplishments led to his earning the nickname of "Mister America's Cup" and being named to the America's Cup and U.S. Sailing Halls of Fame.

Within the yachting community, Conner is most famous for looking to the horizon and fundamentally changing the America's Cup, and racing in general, from an amateur to professional status.

Before the 1980s, America's Cup competitors were mostly amateurs who took time off to compete. Conner, a former Olympic medalist, insisted on year-round training with a new focus on physical fitness and practice. This change in approach led to a return to professional crews in sailing, which had hardly been seen since the 1930s.

Conner successfully defended the Cup in 1974 and 1980. But, in the words of author Marshall Goldsmith, sometimes what got you here won't get you there. In 1983 he was the skipper of the first defender to be defeated in the 132-year history of the Cup, also ending 132 years of successful defense by the New York Yacht Club.

For the first 132 years of America's cup the sport was static and progress came gradually. However, the technological revolution changed that.

Connor did not give up or choose to live in the glory days of the past. Instead he looked to the future and changed strategy.

Following the 1983 loss Conner formed his own syndicate, the Sail America Foundation, through which he raised funds to mount a challenge. Representing the San Diego Yacht Club, he embarked upon a three-year campaign, which culminated in his winning the Cup back from Australia in 1987. He capped off his comeback story by winning the Cup for a fourth time in 1988.

What will the future hold in your industry? Who can say? But one thing is certain: the only constant is change. Build into your smooth selling system the ability to scan the horizon for the changes that are coming your way.

Chris Wooten's Story

One organization that needed to take a different sales tack was NICE Systems, founded in 1986 as Neptune Intelligence Computer Engineering (NICE) by seven Israeli ex-army colleagues. The company initially focused on developing solutions for security and defense applications, but soon looked to the horizon.

A decision was made to refocus the company's efforts on civilian applications, mainly for contact center, financial services, and business intelligence markets. This continually scanning the horizon eventually helped the company reach the $1 billion in revenues milestone in 2013.

Along the way Chris Wooten, the general manager, and I were able to bring a smooth selling system to NICE Systems. Wooten, a career corporate level sales executive with communication technology products, including Motorola, brought me in as a senior sales director for North America. When we took the helm we decided the organization needed to come about and take a new selling direction.

With a few maneuvers NICE Systems achieved smooth selling. Together our team increased the sales pipeline by 332 percent (to $35.8 million) over a three-year period.

Here is the different tack Wooten and I took. NICE Systems had a sales organization that was selling direct to the end user and also supporting a channel of wholesale resellers. Our sales people were being asked to be all things to all people. The problem is direct sales people are hunters and channel support people are farmers.

The underlying issue is hunters are closers, not mentors. Hunters are ego driven and want to control the sale. To support a reseller channel, the sales people need to subordinate their egos and coach the channel so they can close sales on their own. Farmers get satisfaction from helping others succeed.

Hunters need to be measured on the sales they close, while farmers are partially gauged on how well they prepare their reseller channels to sell with little to no assistance from them. In fishing parlance, farmers teach others to fish and hunters go fishing to catch fish.

Unfortunately, many people at NICE Systems did not fit either role of hunter or farmer. As part of a sales reorganization we had to bring in new people that fit the roles. On top of that we kept the roles distinct and did not make a sales person try to be both hunter and farmer.

Then we segmented the market so the direct sales hunters could focus their efforts on bigger opportunities that the reseller channel did not have a chance of penetrating. Our farmers helped the resellers focus on the mid-market, which was where the better opportunities were for them.

As a result, our direct sales team was no longer competing with the reseller channel for business. In the past there was conflict and each group thought the other was stealing their opportunities. After the reorganization there was a noticeable improvement in relationships and lines of communication.

Each quarter we monitored the progress and the strategy. Over the course of the three years we were able to increase annual sales from $4.7 million to $23.1 million, while boosting sales productivity by 65 percent. The key was not just to put in a smooth selling system, but to make the adjustments to keep the selling going smoothly.

And in Closing

If you are struggling with sales, you are not alone. Here are some of the statements I often hear from business leaders.

"My sales have been at the same level for years and I can't get them to the next level."

"I can't find the right sales people and I want to stop the revolving door."

"I'm forced to ignore the rest of my business because I am spending too much time managing the company's sales efforts."

Just remember that in any organization, it is the job of leadership to enable the organization to close more sales, close them faster, and to predictably grow sales year after year by designing and deploying the right sales infrastructure needed to achieve significant growth. Is it the ineffective handling of prospective deals resulting in squandered sales opportunities? Or is it a scarcity of qualified prospective deals that results in a disappointing lack of anticipated growth?

Whatever the challenge, the solution is within these pages. Please reach out to me if I can offer clarity on these concepts and how to put them into practice. Also, please share with me your success stories so I may relay them to my audiences and readers. I wish you all the best as you strive to create a system that will ensure for your company smooth selling forever.

Appendix

A. Smooth Selling Forever Toolkit

Strategic Sales Planning Tools

- ☐ Planning Process Tool
- ☐ Strategy Checklist
- ☐ Market Analyzers
    - SWOT Analysis
    - PESTLE Analysis
- ☐ Competitor Analyzer
- ☐ Channel Assessment Checklist
- ☐ Grading Your Customers Worksheet
- ☐ Ideal Customer Profile Worksheet
- ☐ Functional Buying Persona Worksheet
- ☐ Territory Evaluation Tool
- ☐ Territory Design Tool
- ☐ Value Proposition Creation Tool
- ☐ 5 x 5 Sales Growth Strategies Worksheet

Sales Enablement Tools

- ☐ Staffing and Hiring Tools
- ☐ Hiring Process Template
- ☐ Candidate Filtering/Screening Questionnaire
    - Team Role Worksheet
    - Interview Evaluation Tool
    - Talent Assessment Tool
    - Job Description Template
    - Offer Letter Template
- ☐ Sales Training Tools
    - New Hire Training Program Tool
    - Sales Training Adoption Program Tool
    - Sales Rep Onboarding Checklist
    - Sales Call Coaching Tool
- ☐ Sales/Buying Process Development Tool
- ☐ Goal Setting & Budgeting Tools
    - Goals & Action Planning Tool
    - 1-Year Goal Setting Tool
    - Quota Setting Tool
    - Sales Projection & Forecasting Tool
    - Targeting Analysis Tool
    - Opportunity Evaluator
    - Funnel Math Worksheet
    - Sales Performance Measurement Tools

☐ Weekly Sales Scorecard
- Weekly Activity Report
- Weekly Opportunity Report
- Performance Evaluation Tool

☐ CRM Questionnaire for Assessing Needs

☐ Sales Compensation
- Compensation Best Practices Guide
- Written Compensation Plan Template
- Compensation Plan Spreadsheet

☐ Sales Meetings
- Team Meeting Agenda Template
- 1-2-1 Meeting Agenda Template

B. Sales Team Role Worksheet

Sales Team Role: ________________________________

Responsibilities:

- ________________________________
- ________________________________
- ________________________________
- ________________________________
- ________________________________

Authority:

- ________________________________
- ________________________________
- ________________________________
- ________________________________
- ________________________________

Accountable / Performance Metrics:

- Activity or Result________________________________
- Activity or Result________________________________
- Activity or Result________________________________
- Activity or Result________________________________
- Activity or Result________________________________

C. Job Candidate Profile

Experience:

- ____
- ____
- ____
- ____
- ____

Skills:

- ____
- ____
- ____
- ____
- ____

Personality Traits:

- ____
- ____
- ____
- ____
- ____

D. Interview Evaluation Tool

Candidate: ______________________________

Date: ______________________________

Characteristic	Characteristic Weight	Score	Weighted Score
industry sales experience			
understanding of the development environment			
sales track record			
sales cycle fit			
sales transaction size fit			
formal sales training			
income fit			
personality fit			

Characteristic Weight:

3= Critical
2 = a Plus
1 = a basic need

Scoring:

3 = Exceeds Expectations
2 = Meets Expectations
1= Short of Expectations
0 = Lacks Characteristic

E. Sales Performance Metrics

				Established Rep		
		Sales Performance Metric	Time period Measured	Target	Minimum Acceptable	Annual Target
ACTIVITY	1					
	2					
	3					
	4					
RESULTS	5					
	6					
	7					
	8					

F. Sales Meeting Agenda

Good News (10 minutes)

- Success Stories / Won Deals
- What's Working

Reporting (5 minutes)

- Sales Scorecard Review
- Resource Check-in

To-Dos (5 minutes)

Issues (30 minutes) – could include sales skills, process or

- Product training
- Conclude (5 minutes)
- To Do Recap
- Communication to company
- Rate Meeting (1–10)

G. Funnel Math Worksheet

	Monthly	Weekly (48 work weeks)	Daily	Quarterly (240 work days)	Annually
Sales Quota (as assigned)	$10,000	$2,500	$500	$30,000	$120,000
Average Revenue Per Sale (historical data or assumption)	$2,500	$2,500	$2,500	$2,500	$2,500
# of Sales to Reach Quota (MRC Quota ÷ Average Dollar Sale)	4.00	1.00	0.20	12.00	48.00
Opportunity to Close Ratio (historical data or assumption)	30.0%	30.0%	30.0%	30.0%	30.0%
Opportunities Required (# of Sales to reach Quota ÷ Close Ratio)	13.33	3.33	0.67	40.00	160.00
# of Sales Meetings Required to Achieve Quota (# of Opportunities Required x # Sales Meetings needed per Qualified Opportunity)	40.00	10.00	2.00	120.00	480.00
# of Sales Meetings Needed to Close a Qualified Opportunity (historical data or assumption)	3	3	3	3	3
# of Prospecting Calls needed to identify an Opportunity (historical data or assumption)	10	10	10	10	10
Average # of Opportunities per Account (historical data or assumption)	2	2	2	2	2
Number of Prospecting Calls	200	50	10	600	2400

Input Numbers

Static Numbers

Output/Computed Numbers

Acknowledgements

Writing this book has been both a labor of love and source of pain. I'm so happy that I can share my story and what I've learned over the past three decades, with the hope that I will positively impact the life of those who are responsible for significant, predictable, and sustainable sales growth in their organization. It has also been in many ways painful to put down on paper what I've learned. I'm a sales guy, for goodness sakes, and like many sales professionals would prefer to talk than write.

I would like to first thank my Lord and Savior, Jesus Christ, for putting me on a life's journey of learning and sharing. Without his wisdom–along with an occasional kick in the pants–this book would never have been written.

My family is the center of my universe: my wife Peg, daughters Shanon and Erin, and of course you, Dad. Your unconditional love, support, and patience are truly mind-blowing to a workaholic like me.

To my Vistage colleagues, you have offered me unbelievable advice and support. Thank you for being who you are. And Dick Smith, my Vistage Chair, supporter, educator, connector, confidant, and friend, thank you for going the extra mile on my behalf. To all of my clients and past employers thank you for paying me to learn on the job; without your counsel, patience, and willingness to give me the helm to your company's sales yacht, this book could never have been written. I owe you more than you will ever know. Over the decades, I've had the privilege of learning from and interacting with people that drastically changed the trajectory of my life and career: Brad Sugars, Verne Harnish, Larry Wilson, Keith Cunningham, and Jeffrey Gitomer. I'm eternally indebted to you.

And last, but not least, my esteemed book editor and publisher, Henry DeVries, the co-founder and CEO of Indie Books International. Henry, you rocked my world and enabled me to do what I was destined to do: write this book. Your knowledge of the book business, guidance, encouragement, patience, personality, and editing skill made the writing and publishing of *Smooth Selling Forever* a pleasurable voyage. Your love of baseball didn't hurt either. I can't wait to get started with you on the *Smooth Selling Forever* template workbook.

About the Author

Craig Lowder is a sales-effectiveness expert with a thirty-year track record of helping owners of small and mid-size companies achieve their sales goals. He is the president of MainSpring Sales Group, which assists businesses in need of a strategic sales leader on a part-time contract or project basis to develop and execute a sales strategy, develop sales process and performance management systems, and ensure sales execution. Lowder has worked with over fifty companies and increased first-year annual sales from 22 to 142 percent.

For the majority of his career, Lowder has served in senior sales leadership and advisory roles. His expertise includes sales-strategy development, sales-channel management, sales operations, and marketing. His experience spans a variety of B2B and B2C industries, such as retail, manufacturing, capital management, information technology, software, and business services. He has worked for three Fortune 100 companies: Monsanto, Lucent, and CenturyLink.

He speaks extensively on the topics "Smooth Selling Forever" and "Your Sales Should Run Like Clockwork" for Vistage International, the world's largest CEO peer-to-peer association, and other groups and associations.

Lowder is a 2011 recipient of the President's Discretionary Award in the category of Focus / Prepare / Communicate as a Sales Enablement Consultant for CenturyLink, the 2010 Ownership COACH Action Man Award from a 300-plus member peer group, and the 2003 Early Stage Investment Conference Business Plan Award from the Chicago Software Association. In 2001 he served as chairperson of the National Business Alliance, the vendor advisory group to the 8,000-member National Emergency Number Association Board of Directors

Lowder received his BA degree in marketing from Bradley University and his MBA from DePaul University.

For more information on bulk-order discounts of this book or to learn more about hiring Lowder as a keynote or workshop speaker, please e-mail clowder@mainspringsales.com or call 630-649-4943.